Living

with a ...

GANGSTA

Charlie Mills

Living

with a...

GANGSTA

Charlie Mills

NEW HOLLAND

To my eternally patient parents

This edition first published in 2008 by New Holland Publishers (UK) Ltd
London • Cape Town • Sydney • Auckland
www.newhollandpublishers.com
10 9 8 7 6 5 4 3 2 1

Garfield House, 86–88 Edgware Road, London, W2 2EA, United Kingdom
80 McKenzie Street, Cape Town, 8001, South Africa
Unit 1, 66 Gibbes Street, Chatswood, NSW 2067, Australia
218 Lake Road, Northcote, Auckland, New Zealand

ISBN 978 1 84773 275 0

Senior Editor: Kate Parker
Editorial Direction: Rosemary Wilkinson
Illustrations: Tom Hughes
Cover design: Zoe Mellors and Tom Hughes
Design: Zoe Mellors
Production: Melanie Dowland

Reproduction by Pica Digital PTE Ltd, Singapore
Printed and bound in Malaysia by Times Offset (M) Sdn Bhd

CONTENTS

WHAT IS A GANGSTA?

And what has happened to my teenager?

Here is the brutal truth: not everyone finds your life as exciting as you do. Particularly not the gangsta-posing teenager you have living with you – all he cares about are fast cars, designer clothes and dirty cash. You may have noticed this is causing a spot of friction at home, but don't worry, this book is here to help you understand these new developments.

Perhaps you feel rejected that your resident Gangsta is behaving oddly. Try to see things from his point of view. Honestly, if you had the choice, would you choose your sensible Ford Focus over a Hummer with fat exhausts that goes like a tiger? Would you really opt to be an ISA-saving worrier when you could be splashing out on champagne worth more than your house? And if being so incredibly flash involved very attractive people of the opposite sex shaking their wares at you, and all you had to do in return was talk along to a bass-heavy record while wearing an unfeasible amount of jewellery, would you really not be tempted to give it a go?

Well, your teenager is and he's bought into this gangsta lifestyle hook, line and sunglasses. Being a rapper is a life of rich pickings and non-stop excitement. The fact he is currently trapped in a comfortable suburban existence just makes the gangsta paradise gleam a bit more brightly. He reckons he will score massive reeee-spect at school if he's the one who sees beyond the end of their little National Curriculumed world into a bigger, blingier one.

No one can deny you did your best for him. You bought his shoes from Clarks so his feet would grow wide and true. You read him stories to inspire him to greatness, played quality music to him in the womb and even took him to the odd museum. You helped him with his homework even after a hard day's work yourself.

But now he is speaking a whole new language you don't even understand and he seems to have adopted a new walk that makes your eyeballs ache. The music he has found online gives you an intense headache that pills alone cannot shake.

Blame the school, blame the music, blame yourself for all the unchecked hours he spent watching the girls in gold hotpants on MTV. Do all that if you must, but the only way to really help you make sense of this unnerving situation is to understand exactly what is going through Gangsta's head. Read on...

HOW TO SPOT A
Gangsta

If you are waiting for the moment Gangsta sits you down at the kitchen table and says, 'Mum, Dad, I'm a Gangsta now,' you will be hanging around forever. Cut to the chase with this helpful quiz...

		YES	NO
1	If he were a DVD, would he come with his own Parental Advisory sticker?	☐	☐
2	Does he use the letter 'g' very sparingly, as in 'watchin', 'lovin' or 'vacuumin'?	☐	☐
3	Does he appear to walk with some physical discomfort, yet shun your offer to take him to the chiropodist?	☐	☐
4	Is he in the habit of wearing clothes several sizes too big for him?	☐	☐
5	Does his jewellery make him resemble Mr T more than is appropriate for one who is not an official member of The A-Team?	☐	☐

		YES	**NO**

6	If you were to borrow his iPod and actually make some sense from the incomprehensible lyrics, would they make you blush?	❑	❑
7	Do his friends call him by a name that you did not christen him and certainly do not approve of?	❑	❑
8	Has he recently adopted an attitude to women that would make Hugh Hefner look like a feminist?	❑	❑
9	Is he obsessed by having a huge gas-guzzling car that can belch out enough carbon dioxide to turn the last remaining iceberg into a giant Slush Puppie?	❑	❑
10	Has he started referring to your family home as his 'crib'?	❑	❑

If you answered YES to five or more of these, then congratulations! You are living with a Gangsta.

BEING A GANGSTA:
The Rules

RULE 1

Never march briskly along the street when a deliberately slow rolling strut will do. Imagine your kneecap has popped out of place and soon the pain will seem dangerously real. Most importantly, your walk is there to be admired, so give your public time to take a really good look at you.

RULE 2

Use your hands busily as you talk, in the manner of a dyslexic air traffic controller. If you do not look like you are about to dislocate your arm while you snap your fingers and say, 'Yeah, yeah, yeah, yeah, yeah,' you are doing it wrong.

RULE 3

No matter what shape you are – rail thin, chunky or more muscular than King Kong, the same size T-shirt will fit you.

RULE 4

You must be willing to misuse the Queen's English. However deeply embedded your knowledge of grammar and sentence-structure, you must forget it all if you are to be taken seriously. Remember, don't say 'are' if you can say 'is', i.e. NOT 'What are you talking about, mum?' but 'Wat is you talkin' about, woman?'

RULE 5

Begging your parents for money is as easy as breathing for you.
Practise frequently.

RULE 6

At the end of every sentence use the phrase, 'Knaw wat I'm
sayin? Knawat am *sayin?*' Do not be flummoxed by straight-
laced people who respond with, 'No, Gangsta, I'm afraid I have
absolutely no idea what you are trying to say. Please do try to
speak properly.'

RULE 7

Though wearing a 20lb chain around your neck may give you
back problems, you will quickly develop a beefy bulldog neck
and all your suffering will be worthwhile.

RULE 8

If other kids at school see fit to mock you, it is because they
are morons.

RULE 9

Check the bass on your stereo is loud enough by lolloping down
to the end of the street to see if your internal organs are still
vibrating.

RULE 10

You are cooler than everybody else – just as long as you can
fight off the overwhelming desire to spend your Saturday nights
playing Sudoku and sipping a nice cup of Earl Gray.

EVOLUTION OF A GANGSTA

Your darling little soldier was not attacked by the bling monster overnight, oh no. The changes started so gradually it's not surprising you're now baffled by your boy...

STAGE 1

He is a charming little lad who eats his greens, loves his parents and says 'Please' and 'Thank you' without too much prompting. He is happiest playing conkers, watching 'Dr Who' and collecting Top Trumps – innocent pleasures of which you greatly approve. He works hard at school (inspired by your fine example, no doubt) and you can imagine a future together where he saves you from the evil clutches of a retirement home that smells of wee. At Christmas he feels so guilty about getting so many generous presents from you (a magnifying glass AND a comb) that he gives them to charity and begs for you all to go down and help the homeless at the nearest soup kitchen.

STAGE 2

Alas, you have not accounted
for the influence of the big
men on MTV and his friend at
school who starts feeding him
peculiar ideas. He has got it
into his head that there is no
need to spend years working
hard to get a nice house and
a life of simple pleasures,
because if he was a gangsta,
he would be tough enough to
get mega-rich in a minute. He
sees men on the TV dripping
with gold and fur coats and
he's noticed their fancy cars in
the background and – how
could he not? – the women
hanging around. If he had
that much cash, all that could
be his. If you refuse to
finance his gangsta fantasy,
he will rap his way to riches.
Late at night you hear him
talking to himself in what you
assume is tongues.

STAGE 3

When he returns from a shopping expedition you notice his clothes are all XXL, though he remains the same boyish size. 'Who da maaan?' he asks, eyes bright with excitement. 'Me?' you reply, pretty sure you have not got the correct answer. His sunglasses come down like shutters, signalling the end of your contribution to the conversation. Oh dear. Now is not the time to ask whether he has done his homework. You decide not to mention that it is not common practice to wear sunglasses indoors unless you accessorise them with a white cane. He is wearing a T-shirt with Gothic lettering across the chest. Could it be down to that novel collection he got for Christmas? You are momentarily pleased by this interest in 18th-century literature, until you realise the weird font is just so you cannot easily read the filth spelt out by the Gothic letters. Upstairs, the music coming from his room gets louder.

STAGE 4

'Have your people talk to my people,' he says when you politely ask if he will be in for supper. You are not sure who his people are exactly, or what he can be doing that means he is out on a school night. Later, you overhear him and his friends talking about women as if they might have had some experience in that field, but you cannot think when this can have occurred. He is devoting more time to the development of his 'sound', which means his music is now playing at a volume somewhere above deafening. You cannot decipher the lyrics but he certainly sounds pretty angry. About what? Never having to struggle for anything in his whole cushy life?

STAGE 5

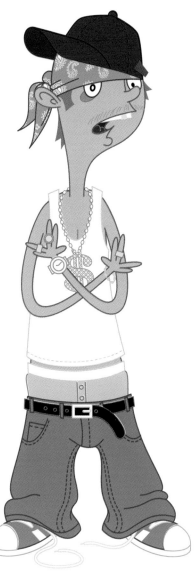

You are starting to think he might have rabies as he mutters in a language you do not understand, holds his arms at funny angles and cannot walk in a straight line. Then, just as you decide to take him to the doctor's, something amazing happens. The unintelligible music video he uploads on YouTube becomes an international internet phenomenon. He becomes the prize in a record label bidding war and when you open the paper you realise he is suddenly worth several million pounds. You try to keep him grounded by insisting he finishes his homework before leaving the house but his seven foot, beef-mountain bodyguard tells you that will not be possible because Gangsta has girls to meet and autographs to sign.

LIVING WITH A GANGSTA:
DOs and DON'Ts

DOs

1   DO correct his grammar as if his life depends on it. (It does, in a way. If he continues to refer to women as 'da laydeez' in adulthood, he will be lucky to escape a good hiding from the local Women's Institute.)

2   DO upgrade your sensible family car to a nice big Hummer because then Gangsta will treat you with serious respect. What do you mean you can't afford it!

3   DO fiddle with the controls on his stereo so it plays nothing but Radio 4. A dose of 'Woman's Hour' and 'The Today Programme' will go some way to repairing the damage gangsta rap has done to his IQ.

4   DO encourage him to work some calming yoga mantras into his rap routine. It will calm him down and help him find inner peace. Ommmmmm.

5   DO try and persuade him to join forces with the Royal National Institute For Deaf People because his demonstrative hand signals are valuable additions to the standard sign language vocabulary.

6   DO be prepared to take back all your scathing comments about his rapping abilities if he gets a record deal equivalent to a lottery jackpot.

7   DO remind him that the richest and most successful gangstas are known for lavishing expensive gifts upon their families.

8   DO give him a bottle of champagne to pass on to his teacher for Christmas if you wish her to look favourably upon his attitude to work.

9   DO frame that photograph of Gangsta playing the angel Gabriel in his primary school nativity play so you can focus on it during hard, halo-less times.

10   DO buy him a copy of Nigella's *How To Be A Domestic Goddess*, because even the hardest man on the street loves an iced fairy cake.

DON'Ts

1. DON'T re-christen your moggie 'Snoop Catt' to humour Gangsta. She will be laughed out of the neighbourhood and you will spend your retirement fund on pet psychologist fees.

2. DON'T take it personally when he walks straight past you on the street as if he has never met you before, let alone shared a bathroom with you. Behind his thick shades, he would be hard pushed to pick his own reflection out of a line-up.

3. DON'T humour him when he informs you that his name, Simon, is now spelt $imon.

4. DON'T let him slug a fizzy drink straight from the can. How slovenly. Insisting he decant it into a fine bone china cup and saucer and sip it delicately will set him squarely on the path to good manners.

5. DON'T think you will score any favours by telling him he is not a Gangsta, he's a very naughty boy. Especially if said in front of his friends.

6. DON'T tell his friends that before he morphed into Gangsta, he showed exceptional skill in tap-dancing lessons. His *Riverdance* days are behind him now.

7   DON'T let him get behind the wheel of any vehicle more powerful than a bumper car. Yes, Sainsbury's carpark after hours might be an unlikely place to have an accident but when Gangsta attempts to execute a high-speed 90 degree turn, you know it will end in tears. Yours.

8   DON'T leave your credit card lying around unless you are as well-to-do as Bill Gates.

9   DON'T tolerate bad language in your home. Unless it passes through your own fair lips, of course.

10   DON'T even bother buying him any item of clothing that does not come with a well-known label. The fact that the garment is made in the same Chinese factory as items a fraction of the price should not be thrust up Gangsta's nose if you are interested in staying alive until suppertime.

INSIDE A GANGSTA'S BEDROOM:

A Spotter's Guide

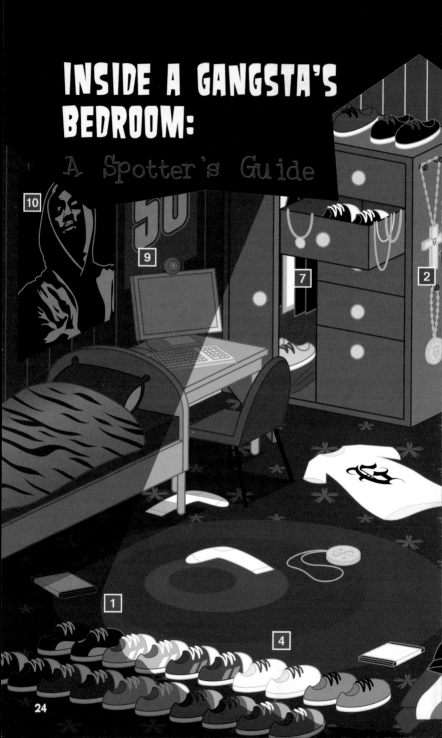

1   Mood lighting **Low-lit his bedroom may be, but this is an energy-saving-lightbulb free zone. He is aiming for the dark, seductive light of über-exclusive VIP areas frequented by 50 Cent and, um, Prince Harry. He must have seen photographs of such club lounges because there is no way he could know what goes on in there for real. (Could he! *Could he?* Please God, let it not be so.)**

2   Jewellery **With all that bling lying around, you could be confused for thinking you were in a nightmare version of Aladdin's cave. In fact, Gangsta has simply raided the chunky section of Claire's Accessories and taken home everything that glitters.**

3   Mirror **For now, the mirror remains on the wall. It is only time before it graduates to the ceiling. Shudder.**

4   Rows of trainers **They look like something straight out of the Tate Modern, lined up so beautifully. You may well wonder why he requires so many expensive pairs of shoes that look exactly the same.**

5   Sound system **When you realise just how big that speaker is, do you honestly wonder why Gangsta has become so deaf to your voice! He is practically living in a speaker and his whole body vibrates with the bass.**

6   DVD library **It's no wonder your local Blockbuster is having a hard time staying in business – Gangsta has a wider range of knock-off DVDs stacked up here than that little man in the dodgy jacket who accosted you outside Tesco.**

7   Wardrobe **He refers to his clothes as 'urban wear', so it should not be a surprise to discover there are no deerstalkers hats or waxy Barbour jackets lurking in here. They are country wear, fool.**

8   Dirty pile of unspecified items **Cover your eyes, walk away and pretend you never saw the flies circling over that pile unless you want nightmares.**

9   Webcam **All the better for rapping into, my dear. When he achieves worldwide fame and untold wealth through the magic of Bebo and YouTube, his fans will forever recognise the shabby backdrop of his bedroom. You will wish you had finally got round to Polyfilling that crack in the paintwork before the whole ruddy world saw it and assumed you lived in squalor.**

10 Posters of double-hard men. **It's hard to get your head around the kind of guys Gangsta looks up to. They look menacing enough to make you cry for your mother, yet there's no way these men can be so groomed without salon-based professional help. Is the 'macho manicure' the look of the future?**

THE GANGSTA TRANSLATA

Wag wan, sucka? Me be da hardass supafly in da crib, blud.

It is a struggle to understand what Gangsta is trying to say. You can just about cope with the odd dropped 'g' or 'h', but he seems to have developed a whole new range of vocabulary that is beyond your comprehension.

Fortunately, the basics are translated right here for you:

Badass über-cool or awesome to the highest level, thus scoring unquestionable authority. Precisely what Gangsta aspires to be.

Biatch A substitute for 'bitch' when the politeness police are on patrol.

Blud Acknowledgement of a close friend in his gang. Unlikely to be used in reference to you, sadly, even though you are genuine 'blood'.

Butterface Used in reference to a woman in possession of an undeniably impressive body but a face that would scare horses. So, everything 'but her face' is attractive.

Douche bag A person who talks rubbish and is annoying. For reasons unknown, this is related to a rarely-used vaginal cleaning practice.

Face An exclamation used after a person has been humiliated, as in, 'In your face'. For example, if Gangsta's *Brain Training* age is superior to yours he might shout, 'Face!' and make you feel about five centimetres high.

Fugly The politest possible way Gangsta can think of to describe a person who is fucking ugly. He deserves a little credit for that, no?

Hardass One who believes they are tough. With Gangsta's current poor arm-wrestling prowess, it is imperative he finds a pack of bodyguards immediately.

Haters People who find it impossible to be happy for Gangsta's success. Try harder, you miserable old halibut.

Hoe A garden implement, you say? Not any more. To Gangsta, it means a promiscuous person.

Hustler One who has a knack of getting money from others. Wise up to it or start working out how you can live on a budget diet of baked beans.

Killer Nothing to do with Jack The Ripper. For some reason, 'killer' means 'very, very cool' in Gangsta-speak.

Mother-fudger Think about it... Then move on, quickly.

Phat It is pronounced 'fat' but it stands for 'Pretty Hot And Tempting' so consider it a compliment and cancel your subscription to Weight Watchers. However, 'phat' is not the cool word it once was and is now considered something of a slangy faux pas.

Playa One who is outgoing and competitive enough to get noticed for playing a good game. This usually refers to sexual relations with the opposite sex, not Scrabble-based skills.

Sick Cool. The days 'sick' referred to vomit and its bacteria-rich associations are over.

Sup A contraction of the phrase, 'What is up?' though you are not expected to reply with anything that might cause the gangsta to break his stride, such as, 'Your cat died today.' Keep it light, please.

Sucka A weakling who should acknowledge you are superior to him.

Supafly Suave, intelligent, sophisticated, charming and respected. Sound like anyone you know?

Thug A person going through a struggle. Like Gordon Brown, for example.

Wag wan An easy way of saying 'What is going on?' for people with speech impediments.

Wife beater A vest worn when all Gangsta's favourite T-shirts are in the wash.

GANGSTA:

Let the music be your guide

When you understand gangsta rap you will get to the very core of Gangsta's being.

Start treasuring all those occasions he rolls his eyes in horror at your uncoolness because they are soon to be a thing of the past. Here you will find helpful suggestions of lyrics to quote in specific situations – Gangsta will sit up and listen. Wearing a pair of sunglasses and moving your hands as the mood takes you will help develop your own rapping style. Good luck.

Is Gangsta hard to wake up for school in the morning? Help him resist the temptation to live the rest of his life under the duvet with a few rousing lines from Tupac:

'You know what time, boo-yaow
I know it's time for you
So grab one by the hand youknowhatl'msayin
And uhh, throw up that finger
Ay yo yo yo throw y'all fingers up!
Thug style baby, thug style y'know?'

Tupac, 'Temptations'

When you are trying to show Gangsta how far-reaching your influence on the world is, quote this. The last line will prove exactly how wise and in touch with nature you are...

'Picture me, pen in hand writin' lines knowin' the Source'll quote it
When I die, they'll read this and say a genius wrote it
I grew up without my Pops, should that make me bitter?
I caught cases I copped out, does that make me a quitter?
In this white man's world, I'm similar to a squirrel.'

50 Cent, 'Patiently Waiting'

Do you ever feel the need to remind Gangsta the world is a beautiful place and he actually does not have that much to moan about! Try this:

'Have a look outside, take a stroll with me
California lifestyle, you want to roll with me?
I can take you in and out, What's it gonna be?
Now as crazy as it is, you know its home for me
I would never leave it, you know that's wrong to me.'

Snoop Dogg, 'Crazy'

Do you think Gangsta Girl has moved your cheese? Show her who is boss in the refrigerator department with these choice lines:

'When you frown at me is it because I won't provide for you girl
You're after me chedda
And your friends they see it to screaming we know what you're up to girl
I'm after my chedda.'

G Unit, 'After My Chedda'

WHAT NOT TO SAY
to a Gangsta

Gangsta can be a little temperamental
so it is best not to wind him up
wherever possible.

When you feel one of these trigger
phrases on the tip of your tongue,
try to hold back...

'What's this
music? Is it
that
Eminenema
having a
moan
again?'

'Please can I
borrow some
money?'

'Ooh, nice
earrings.
Where can
I get a
fancy pair
like that?'

'I've decided to trade in our car for a loom so I can weave all our clothes.'

'I ain't saying you're a golddigga, but...'

'MC HAMMER CALLED. HE WANTS HIS TIME BACK.'

'I think you need to practise a little Buddhist meditation to calm you down, pal.'

'Do you remember when you were President of the Junior Ornithologist's Club? I do...'

'I am worried about you. I've booked us a family therapy appointment with Dr Quackenbush.'

'IT'S HIGH TIME WE DID SOMETHING TOGETHER, AS A FAMILY. HOW'S ABOUT WE ALL HEAD DOWN TO THE BARN DANCE ON SATURDAY NIGHT?'

'Is that Grandma's gold locket you're wearing around your neck!'

'I know you love music, so I've enrolled you in a musical theatre workshop. Jazz hands, woo!'

'I DON'T CARE IF YOU'RE DUE AT THE MTV STUDIOS, YOU'RE GROUNDED!'

'I can see your pants.'

'I'm having a few relationship problems of my own. Got any advice?'

GANGSTA STYLE AND GROOMING

He's definitely working 'A look' but can you bear to cast your eyes over it?

So much effort goes into orchestrating Gangsta's look that you have to admire him for it, even if you are not sure what sort of style statement he is trying to make. Fortunately, this list might help break it down for you...

BASEBALL CAP

HAIR

SMILE

HOODIE

T-SHIRT

UNMISTAKABLE ODOUR

JEWELLERY

JEANS

TRAINERS

£69.99

39

Jeans Even brainiacs like Stephen Hawking, the world's foremost theoretical physicist, cannot get their heads around the peculiarity of Gangsta's jeans. How is it that the waistband sits *below* the buttocks, and yet the jeans do not fall to the ankle? Forget, if you can, the question of why one would choose to expose their underwear. How do those jeans stay up? The principles of physics cannot explain the mystery. Is Gangsta magic at work!

T-shirt It is big enough to clothe your whole family. What possible reason might he have for wearing such a vast mainsail of a garment when he is not nearly big enough to fit it? Is he wearing it that large in protest at the European Clothing Mountain? Maybe he is planning a sit-in at the Mars factory and will not go quietly until he has eaten every chocolate bar on the premises? It is a mystery.

Hoodie In an age when so many teenagers insist on exposing too much goosepimpled flesh in our cool climate, you have to give Gangsta a point for keeping warm in a ginormous sweatshirt. However, you must warn him that his insistence on wearing it even in searing heat is surely bad for his health.

Trainers Despite the comfort of his Air Jordans, Gangsta walks with a pimp limp. His trainers have no sporting purpose. In fact, being so oversized and loosely-laced, his little feet would pop straight out if he were to ever try bursting into a sprint.

Jewellery **They call it 'bling' apparently. Your treasured family jewels that have been lovingly passed down the generations for hundreds of years – but crucially never worn – have now been melted down by Gangsta and turned into a golden bicycle chain for his neck.**

Baseball cap **For some reason that continues to elude laws of style and common sense, he has kept the sales tag on his baseball cap so he persistently looks like he is shoplifting. Frankly, you are surprised that any shop would dare to charge more than 30 pence for a silly cap like that anyway.**

Hair **Heck, for the amount of times you have seen it recently, he could be bald as a billiard ball underneath that hat.**

Unmistakable odour **It is not the scent of wet dog that follows Gangsta around, but rather a very expensive cologne by mogul rapper Sean John, called 'Unforgivable'. The name is savagely appropriate.**

Smile **You keep meaning to tell Gangsta he has a big bit of foil stuck in his teeth, but you can never find the right moment. What you don't want to know is that his shiny tooth is as permanent as the sun in the sky, and twice as bright. When you drag him along to visit Granny at Christmas, beg him to keep his mouth shut.**

GANGSTA:

Let the music be your guide

Gangsta can take an annoyingly long time preening in the bathroom every morning, which causes serious strain on your bladder. If you need the loo as a matter of urgency, rap this as you hammer on the door:

'I got 21 seconds to flow
I got 21 seconds to go
Cause if you like me let me know
Let me in the studio
I got 21 seconds before I got to go.'

So Solid Crew, '21 Seconds'

Having a mid-life crisis? You might feel better talking to Gangsta about it...

'As I walk through the valley of the shadow of death
I take a look at my life and realize there's nothing left
Cause I've been blastin' and laughing so long that
Even my mama thinks that my mind is gone.'

Coolio, 'Gangsta's Paradise'

You have no deep, hidden message here. You just want to show Gangsta how very flash you are...

'I was like, good gracious ass bodacious
Flirtatious, tryin' to show patience
Lookin' for the right time to shoot my steam (you know)
Lookin' for the right time to flash them G's
Then um I'm leavin', please believin'
Me and the rest of my heathens
Check it, got it locked at the top of the Four Seasons
Penthouse, roof top, birds I feedin'
No deceivin', nothin' up my sleeve, no teasin''

Nelly, 'Hot In Here'

If you would like a punch in the face, sing this sweet little song:

'She had dumps like a truck, truck, truck
Thighs like what, what, what
Baby move your butt, butt, butt
I think I'll sing it again'

Sisquo, 'Thong Song'

How can we put this delicately? Gangsta has a 'relaxed' attitude towards his schoolwork. Before he condemns himself to a lifetime claiming the dole, encourage him to get through his exams with these wise words:

'Look, if you had one shot, or one opportunity
To seize everything you ever wanted – one moment
Would you capture it or just let it slip?'

Eminem, 'Lose Yourself'

8 REASONS TO RATE GANGSTA GIRLS

Stereotypically, Gangstas are boys. But the female of the species is deadlier than the male, and Gangsta girls exist in their gazillions.

This book just says 'he' for the sake of grammatical correctness. And because 'he or she' takes a yawnsomely long time to type. Sorry about that. Anyway, Gangsta Girls are a force to be reckoned with so it is best you understand her code of conduct, here:

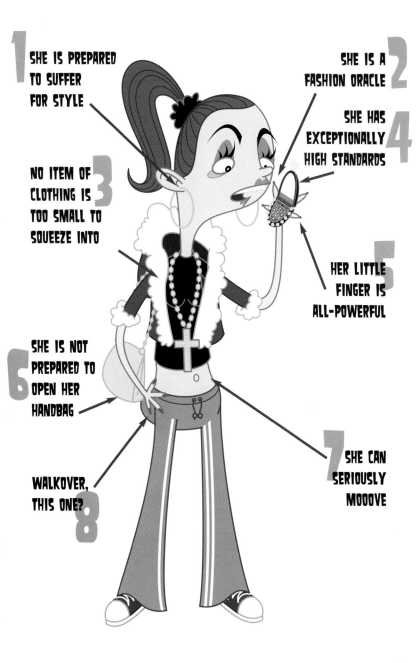

1 SHE IS PREPARED TO SUFFER FOR STYLE

2 SHE IS A FASHION ORACLE

4 SHE HAS EXCEPTIONALLY HIGH STANDARDS

3 NO ITEM OF CLOTHING IS TOO SMALL TO SQUEEZE INTO

5 HER LITTLE FINGER IS ALL-POWERFUL

6 SHE IS NOT PREPARED TO OPEN HER HANDBAG

7 SHE CAN SERIOUSLY MOOOVE

8 WALKOVER, THIS ONE?

1 She is prepared to suffer for style. **In her book, earrings can never be too large. Maybe in 20 years she will look like an elephant, but you suspect she will use this as an opportunity to fit more bling on her lobes.**

2 She is a fashion oracle. **If someone asks, 'What on earth are you wearing young lady?' she will proudly reel off the designer labels covering her back and interpret the sharp, accusatory tone as an envious fashion enquiry.**

3 No item of clothing is too small to squeeze into. **Clothes should be so tight it looks like she has been attacked by felt tips. If she cannot find any garments suitably close-fitting, she should go to McDonalds and not return until she has filled her clothes to bursting.**

4 She has exceptionally high standards. **A mobile phone that is not covered in diamonds (or at least a scattering of stick-on faux crystals) is not worth talking into. Your phone looks like an old Etch-A-Sketch in comparison.**

Her little finger is all-powerful. It is hard to resist the force that insists you be wound round it. Some boys might like to think girls are only there to dance around and look pretty. Not so. Girls are there to tell the boys what to do.

She is not prepared to open her handbag. She does have her own money – she simply prefers to spend other people's. Not just a pretty face, eh? But do you think she would be ok if you adopted this philosophy too?

She can seriously mooove. The way she jiggles her backside is weird, but undeniably impressive. If you cannot dance you may as well go home and worship at the altar of MTV until your every step involves a degree of booty-shaking.

Walkover, this one? Toughness is not an exclusively male trait. Have you seen Gangsta Girl's talons! This is not a woman you want to wrestle with if you value your eardrums, your mind or your life.

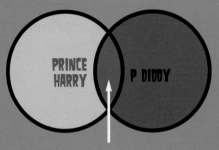

PRINCE
HARRY

P DIDDY

POSH GANGSTA

GANGSTA VENN: POSH GANGSTA

Sod the struggle: for Posh Gangsta, the gangsta lifestyle is non-stop flash-bling-flash-bling, just like P Diddy's. Posh Gangsta wears nothing but the most expensive designer clothes and he has been heard to brag, 'My trainers cost more than your car.' He will never develop a taste for warm cider sipped through gritted teeth on a park bench – like Prince Harry, he goes straight from his mother's milk to champagne in expensive nightclubs. As he grows up, Posh Gangsta is increasingly caught between a nagging feeling of duty, like the ginger Prince in Afghanistan, and a P Diddy-esque belief that he will never get bored of shiny jewellery.

WARNING!

Playin' da Gangsta

A special note on rap merchandise: there is nothing a money-hungry rapper won't do to squeeze another buck out of your Gangsta.

THE GANGSTA'S GANG

You do not have to read The Daily Mail to know that hooded gangs of youths can be intimidating.

Yes, Gangsta's friends are a scary bunch, but as his co-habitee you are in a privileged position: you can join them.

First of all, make it clear they are unwelcome in your home. This guarantees they will elect to hang out in your living room at every opportunity, enabling you to keep an eye on them.

YOU NOTICE GANGSTA REFERS TO ALL OF HIS FRIENDS AS 'BRO' AND FEEL A LITTLE IRKED – HOW CAN THEY BE HIS BROTHERS?

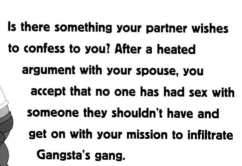

Is there something your partner wishes to confess to you? After a heated argument with your spouse, you accept that no one has had sex with someone they shouldn't have and get on with your mission to infiltrate Gangsta's gang.

Though you are acclimatising to the gang's occupation of your sofa, you cannot get used to the way they never take off their hats and hoods. Fortunately, there is a simple solution: turn the thermostat way, way up and watch the hoods come down.

Now you can see their faces, you feel comfortable enough to make

some polite chit-chat. Discuss how much money you have and how global warming will encourage more women to wear hot pants. You will gain the respect of the most money-obsessed member of the gang and get the ladykiller-wannabes thinking happy thoughts.

If you want to progress up the ladder of the gang, bake the crew a batch of biscuits with smiley faces made out of chocolate chips.

EVEN THE THUGGIEST MEMBER WILL HI-5 YOU IN GRATITUDE AND BEG FOR THE RECIPE.

Only swap it for a lesson on how to perform the gang's secret Freemason-style handshake.

Once the handshake is revealed, you are almost a fully-fledged gang member. Take a moment to ask yourself if this is what you really want, because the next stage involves compulsory scars, tattoos and possibly shaving your head.

Are you brave enough yet?

GANGSTA FLICKS

Popcorn, anyone?

Gangsta loves going to the cinema as much as everyone else, as long as the film depicts gratuitous sex, violence and bring-on-the-bankruptcy spending habits.

Here are a few of his favourite films:

Independence Day	**Dependent On You Until The Day I Die**
Boyz In The Hood	**Toyz Out The Pram**
Aladdin	**A Lad In Endless Trouble**
The Devil Wears Prada	**I'll Wear Prada**
Happy Feet	**Happy Slapper**
The Terminator	**The Sperminator**
How To Lose A Guy In 10 Days	**How To Lose Your Pocket Money In 10 Days**
The Sweetest Thing	**The Sweetest Bling**
Stardust	**I'm A Star, You Are Dust**

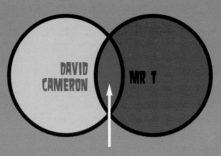

DAVID CAMERON

MR T

CARDBOARD GANGSTA

GANGSTA VENN: CARDBOARD GANGSTA

You cannot quite put your finger on it, but there is something unconvincing about both David Cameron and Cardboard Gangsta. To prove to his brothers that his heart is, like, totally in the gangsta scene, yeah, he gets some jewellery that wouldn't look out of place around Mr T's beefy neck. Unfortunately, his huge gold medallion leaves a weird green mark that just will not shift. Perhaps it is not worth thousands of pounds after all? He lives in fear of being found out and is secretly hoping that gangsta fashion dies off ASAP.

THE FOUR GREAT GANGSTA TRAPS

Get him out of trouble and into line.

TRAP #1: PROJECTING AN IMAGE OF TOUGHNESS

Gangsta is so obsessed with his hard-as-nailclippings reputation that sometimes it appears as if he has lost touch with his feelings. Surely he would be a better human being if he developed his range of emotions?

Rescue operation: **Tie him to a chair and force him to watch *Bambi* until his soft centre spills out through his tear ducts.**

TRAP #2: BAD LANGUAGE

The way Gangsta uses profanities makes your ears bleed. How come it is more socially unacceptable for you to gaffer-tape his mouth than for him to swear every other second?

Rescue operation: **Send him off to Swiss finishing school. As well as deep-cleaning his language, the school will also teach him to get out of a sports car without revealing his underwear – a skill no gangsta can afford to sniff at.**

TRAP #3: REVEALING HIS UNDERWEAR

The trouble with gangsta-style jeans that hang deliberately low is that it is hard to find the right pair of pants to wear underneath. Going commando is not an option (a case of piles in such a young man is nothing short of tragic) but exposing a pair of boxers decorated with dancing Winnie-the-Poohs and Piglets does not cultivate the right image.

Rescue operation: **Braces, obviously. Although mega-rich City gents wear red braces to hold up their trousers, they look a little too Marks & Spencer for Gangsta. However, tell him they cost an unearthly six-figure sum and he will put them on faster than you can say, 'I have no taste but lots of money.'**

TRAP #4: FAILING TO UNDERSTAND WHO IS BOSS

Let's get one thing clear: you are. So why does he demand you fetch and carry for him while simultaneously berating you for not having enough money? You have to admire his ability to turn a situation around, but seeing as you are getting the arse end of the deal, Gangsta needs to be taught a lesson.

Rescue operation: **Reveal the millions you have stashed in offshore bank accounts before escaping the country, leaving Gangsta to pay the mortgage with his paper-round money. If you have no millions, use your last remaining pennies to buy a loudhailer so you can bark orders around the house.**

THE GANGSTA
In Love

For months now, Gangsta has been talking to his friends as if he has had hundreds of girlfriends on the go. Overhearing these snippets is driving you mad as you wrack your brain, trying to remember any occasions when he might have been on a date. Just as you are about to ask your GP whether you might be descending into early-onset Alzheimers, you see her: the girl.

'Ooh, are you courting?' you say as you ambush the pair of them whispering on your doorstep. There is a long silence.

'She's just leaving,' Gangsta says.

'Why don't you ask her over for tea so we can get to know her properly?' you suggest, as the sound of her heels click-clicking down the street recedes. He makes a noise a bit like a snort. Poor lamb, he must be overcome with emotion. Let's not embarrass him.

You hold back, but you cannot help noticing more girls turning up at the house. You aren't spying, honestly, you just noticed the hanging baskets were seriously in need of pruning and the best way to reach them is to scramble onto the porch roof.

The girls are never invited in, but this does not seem to put them off. You are torn between feeling ashamed at his appalling manners and feeling proud that all these young ladies think

your Gangsta is such a catch. Undeniably, they are attracted to him. Gangsta's complete emotional detachment makes him a challenge. All these girls see him as a project that needs fixing. You are inclined to agree.

Gangsta discusses the physical ins and outs of his 'relationships' with his friends. In eye-watering detail. You are worried that his idea of the perfect match is a woman he does not need to talk to or attempt to understand. Then one girl comes along who changes everything: Gangsta transforms into a cuddly puppy, his gang fades into the background and he even gives her his favourite Argos-purchased sovereign ring to show his commitment. You are as pleased to see him happy as you are to get that monstrous piece of jewellery out of your line of vision. Your faith in Happy Ever After is restored.

HOW TO COPE WITH GANGSTA'S

Moods

Gangsta's determination to be king of the castle means he likes to insist on getting his own way just for the sheer hell of it. The trouble is, sometimes you need to have things your way too, at which point Gangsta is likely to throw a pretty intimidating strop...

'Give up already. Go on'

Now is the time to double-check whether you have the stomach to make a stand against letting Gangsta go to an all-night party with people of the opposite sex, the entire stock of Threshers and no parental supervision. Do you really have the stamina to see this fight through?

'Nobody says 'No' to me'

You fool. What did you go and say the n-word for? Gangsta cannot work out why you, his resident minion, are standing in the way of what he wants. Do you realise what you are getting yourself into?

'I promise I will do my homework'

Pleading: nice trick. But shouldn't he be committed to his education for his own benefit, not for yours? After all, he will be the one microwaving cheap hotdogs for a living if he fails his exams. You will not be bribed. Furthermore, he will have more time to devote to his studies if he does not go to the troublesome party.

'I hate you! I hate you! You're gonna regret this until the day you die!'

Them's the breaks, pal. While the blood vessels in Gangsta's head pop with his apocalyptic tantrum, you must hold firm. Tell Gangsta that the best rappers have made millions from writing about their domestic struggles and all you really want is the opportunity for him to do the same. Expect his line, 'I hate you! I hate you! You're gonna regret this until the day you die!' to be on the lips of every teenager in Britain a year from now.

'You are so unfair!'

It's fun being 'unfair', isn't it? You remember when things weren't so fair for you, like when you had to clean up after Gangsta wet the bed. OK, so he was a baby then, but if he goes to this party and gets his mouth around too many alcopops, you could be in for a repeat of that urine-soaked night.

HOW TO EMBARRASS
the Gangsta

If he ever expects to gain respec' in the big bad world, Gangsta needs to toughen up a little. You can fast-track him through the school of hard knocks by making it your mission to embarrass him as much as possible – if he can style these shameful situations out then he is in for a glorious future.

STAGE 1:

When you kiss him goodnight, try and turn the usual peck on the forehead into a souped-up Freemasons / Gangsta handshake. Does he play along?

STAGE 2:

Every time you hear Westlife on the radio, crack your fingers and shout loudly 'This is phaaaat,' before setting the volume to maximum and running out of the room. Is he shuddering?

STAGE 3:

Make him perform his 'music' infront of the old dears at your local nursing home. He won't feel embarrassed to stand up and rap his heart out, will he?

STAGE 4:

Be the first on the dance floor at his birthday party and treat his friends to your special aerobics-inspired routine. You have the magic. Has he got a red face?

STAGE 5:

Insist to his teachers that they should rap out the register to help Gangsta engage with the lesson. Is his cringing palpable?

STAGE 6:

When travelling together on public transport, get out your mobile phone and play a poor-quality recording of something soppy by James Blunt as loudly as possible. Repeat. Repeat again. Has Gangsta thrown himself in the path of the moving vehicle?

STAGE 7:

Drop your trousers as an expression of solidarity. Has he called in the child protection officers?

STAGE 8:

Collect him from school in your new pimped-up ride and drape your gold-hotpanted self across the bonnet as you wait for him to amble out of the gates. Does he greet you with pride?

HAPPY BIRTHDAY,
Gangsta!

For reasons you cannot quite put your finger on, Gangsta seems to want you out of the house for the weekend of his birthday.

'But who will bake you a cake?' you cry. 'Who will blow up balloons and pause the music during Musical Chairs!' Gangsta is openly laughing at you now. Perhaps he has been at the helium already. Whatever. You will not be dissuaded from planning a surprise birthday party for him.

So, in the week leading up to the big day you stand outside the school gate with a bunch of balloons, handing out invitations to nice, clean-cut boys and girls. 'Who's birthday is this?' they all ask.

You forget that your darling little boy has a gangsta name now: that's how they know him. But you cannot help worrying – what if nobody turns up on the night! You take the liberty of hijacking Gangsta's Bebo account and inviting his 739 online friends to come and play.

The morning of his birthday is spent frantically stuffing party bags and scattering chocolate coins on every available surface. You spread metallic gold icing on the cake, hoping that none of the wee children get lead poisoning at your hand. Still, the cake shines like Jimmy Saville's medallion: you are very proud of your efforts.

'Ta da!' you cry, as Gangsta walks into the kitchen, surprised to find you still in the house at all. When he realises what you are up to, he has an unreadable expression of emotion on his face. Gangsta is quite overcome, bless the little lamb. You are determined his party will be a success.

Before Gangsta has a chance to tell you he hates you (he must mean 'love' – you remember he likes things that are 'sick' and that 'wicked' means 'good'), hundreds of unruly teenagers turn up at your house.

NO ONE HEARS YOU POLITELY ASKING FOR THEM TO TAKE THEIR SHOES OFF SO THEY DO NOT SPOIL YOUR LOVELY CREAM CARPET.

Someone wheels in their own mahoosive music system and ignores your suggestion to play a nice quiet game of Sleeping Lions. The whole house rattles with the bass and broken glass rains down from cracked windowpanes. All around you young people are shouting and whooping. And, Heavens, what is *that* noise? A squad of armed police officers break down your front door, handcuff the guests and herd them into riot vans. Still, at least the kids will be able to enjoy their party bags while they wait to be questioned down at the station. Same again next year?

PRESENT WISH-LIST *:

- A copy of the Highway Code, with sections on the dangers of speeding carefully highlighted

- A place at a poetry workshop so I can truly find myself

- Two tickets to the opera. That's what rich people do, innit?

- A pair of boring-looking shoes with correction heels to sort my walk out

- Front row seats to Germaine Greer's cutting-edge lecture series, New Feminism

- A second hand bicycle, to reduce my carbon footprint

* THE AUTHOR CANNOT ACCEPT RESPONSIBILITY FOR GANGSTA'S SATISFACTION WITH THESE GIFTS. YOU FOOL.

THE GANGSTA
On Holiday

There are only a couple of things that can tempt Gangsta away from his busy sofa-and-streets routine at home. Namely, yachts, women, and yachts filled with bikini-clad women. Booyakasha. What do you mean that's not the kind of holiday you have in mind?

GANGSTA HAS SEEN PICTURES OF HIS RAP IDOLS PARTYING ON CARIBBEAN YACHTS, TRASHING PENTHOUSE SUITES AND FLYING ON PRIVATE JETS.

That is what 'holiday' looks like to him. So when you start trying to fob Gangsta off with a week in a sleepy Cornish fishing village, his brain simply does not compute.

'Why haven't you got enough money?' he demands, overlooking the fact that you would be far richer if you were not picking up Gangsta's bills as well as your own. (Incidentally, how is it possible that a teenager has a more expensive lifestyle than you?)

'OK, so what about Vegas?' he says. Bless his optimistic socks. It is hard to explain that even if you had a couple of thousand pounds to throw down the slot machines, you would rather rip off your right arm and let a manky pigeon peck it down to the bone than let Gangsta loose in Las Vegas. Plus, the challenge of getting Gangsta, his jewellery and his attitude through airport security is too much for you to contemplate.

You think some time spent communing with nature and enjoying the simple life will be character-building for Gangsta.

GANGSTA'S PACKING ESSENTIALS:

- Fake ID and a convincing story to explain its existence if Mum finds it

- The biggest pair of speakers I can carry

- A note of Dad's PIN number

- Fifteen pairs of trainers that all look the same

- Mobile phone, so I don't have to speak to anyone I'm actually on holiday with

He will realise that designer labels are meaningless in a world where he can happily lose hours watching waves gently breaking on the shore. He will have the opportunity to actually wear his sunglasses *outdoors*. You know, in the sun. Radical. He might even get a chance to read a book, **something he has not done since the days of *Peter and Jane*.**

Gangsta will relax and may even start to smile involuntarily as he frolics on the pebbly beach.

If Gangsta refuses to join you holidaying in a rustic old cottage with roses around the door, he has an alternative. Namely, the caravan. He could be conned into this idea because he has a vision of hanging out in a luxurious trailer, stuffed with gold and groupies, that is actually bigger than your house. It is worth bringing earplugs for the moment Gangsta sees the mouldy old caravan you expect him to sleep in. Remind him Eminem grew up on a trailer park and you might just get away with it.

When he gets cold and bangs on the door of your cosy holiday cottage in the middle of the night, begging to be let in, be generous.

MAYBE, JUST MAYBE, GANGSTA REALLY WILL SELL MILLIONS OF RECORDS IN THE FUTURE AND CAN TREAT YOU TO A HOLIDAY.

You could see yourself on a private jet, yes? And you wouldn't feel too uncomfortable on a luxury yacht, no?

COMMUNICATION
Tips

Gangsta is not the easiest person in the world to have a conversation with, in case you hadn't noticed.

Take a deep breath and give bonding another go. Try this script to kick-start a meaningful discussion:

'There's a good reason for that. It doesn't fit my image to live with someone so caring and understanding. How about you fake your own death and never contact me again?'

'For you to disappear when I click my fingers'

'I wasn't joking'

'You are talking out of your bottom. What's your PIN number?'

Gangsta seems to be wrestling with a couple of hostility issues. Either send him to compete in 'Gladiators' or pack him off to The Priory for an anger-management course.

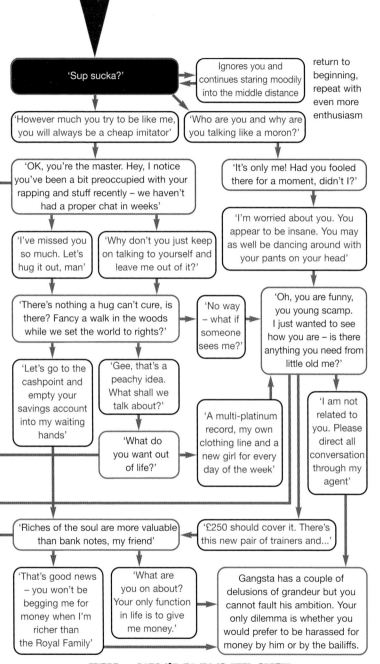

'Sup sucka?'

Ignores you and continues staring moodily into the middle distance

return to beginning, repeat with even more enthusiasm

'However much you try to be like me, you will always be a cheap imitator'

'Who are you and why are you talking like a moron?'

'OK, you're the master. Hey, I notice you've been a bit preoccupied with your rapping and stuff recently – we haven't had a proper chat in weeks'

'It's only me! Had you fooled there for a moment, didn't I?'

'I'm worried about you. You appear to be insane. You may as well be dancing around with your pants on your head'

'I've missed you so much. Let's hug it out, man'

'Why don't you just keep on talking to yourself and leave me out of it?'

'There's nothing a hug can't cure, is there? Fancy a walk in the woods while we set the world to rights?'

'No way – what if someone sees me?'

'Oh, you are funny, you young scamp. I just wanted to see how you are – is there anything you need from little old me?'

'Let's go to the cashpoint and empty your savings account into my waiting hands'

'Gee, that's a peachy idea. What shall we talk about?'

'A multi-platinum record, my own clothing line and a new girl for every day of the week'

'I am not related to you. Please direct all conversation through my agent'

'What do you want out of life?'

'Riches of the soul are more valuable than bank notes, my friend'

'£250 should cover it. There's this new pair of trainers and...'

'That's good news – you won't be begging me for money when I'm richer than the Royal Family'

'What are you on about? Your only function in life is to give me money.'

Gangsta has a couple of delusions of grandeur but you cannot fault his ambition. Your only dilemma is whether you would prefer to be harassed for money by him or by the bailiffs.

THERE – DOESN'T BONDING FEEL GREAT?

WHAT'S GOING ON...

... inside Gangsta's Head?

If I stand next to that Ferrari, everyone will think it's mine.

If it doesn't have bubbles, I'm not drinking it.

When I'm a famous rapper, it's going to look really uncool if anyone finds out I have normal loving parents. I wonder if they accept bribes?

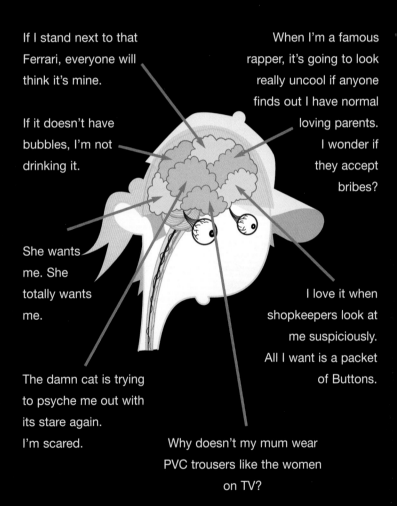

She wants me. She totally wants me.

The damn cat is trying to psyche me out with its stare again. I'm scared.

I love it when shopkeepers look at me suspiciously. All I want is a packet of Buttons.

Why doesn't my mum wear PVC trousers like the women on TV?

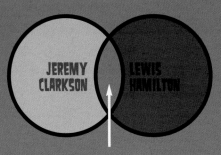

JEREMY CLARKSON

LEWIS HAMILTON

MOTOR-MAD GANGSTA

GANGSTA VENN:
MOTOR-MAD GANGSTA

He shot out of the womb at breakneck speed
and has been driving you mad ever since.
Motor-Mad Gangsta is obsessed with cars and
will do anything to get behind the wheel. But
not just any wheel: a Renault 5 is not
desirable, thank you very much, so stop trying
to fob him off with a cheap old run-around.
Lewis Hamilton would be ashamed to be
papped in that rust-bucket, and so will Motor-
Mad Gangsta – it is no babe-magnet. For some
reason, a passion for cars comes with a sidecar
of misogyny, like the charming Jeremy Clarkson.

THE GANGSTA

In the Future

Assuming that Gangsta does not become a megarich rapper or spend his adult years busily serving time at Her Majesty's Pleasure, he will at some point have to get a proper job and start to earn his own way in the world. Can you imagine...?

Even the coolest rappers eventually hit

30

(Dr Dre must be near pensionable age by now, surely) and if he's not a star by then, perhaps he could consider one of these career options...

POLICEMAN

He is seduced by the glamour of the uniform: the bulletproof vest, the truncheon... ooh, stop. He excels at this job, having had years of practice limping aimlessly around the streets trying to work out how far the law can be pushed.

BUS DRIVER

Gangsta has spent his whole life up to this point dreaming of driving a huge set of wheels around town. Now his dream is fulfilled, but after a succession of speeding tickets he is often found sitting on green at the traffic lights, wondering where it all went wrong.

ESTATE AGENT

He gets to wear a shiny suit, and have people patiently listen to him bragging about what an incredible amount of money he makes. If he wasn't still living at home aged 37, they might take him a little more seriously. One day he might get into the sort of houses he's seen on MTV's 'Cribs', but for now selling semis in Reading will have to do.

DOCTOR

Gangsta's bedside manner laughs in the face of the Hippocratic Oath, but you have to admit he gets results. Rumours that all of his patients exit the hospital with an inexplicable limp are currently unverified. Please, have some respect.

ACCOUNTANT

Money, money, money! If he cannot earn millions of pounds himself, at least let him count it, poor wee thing. And if he gets to wear a pinstripe suit and talk in a language that confuses people who previously believed themselves intelligent, so much the better.

TEACHER

All the respect he could ever ask for is out there, if only he could get those little people in school uniform to stop chatting for two minutes and listen to his rap on simultaneous equations and long division.

CAR DEALER

Like a permanent episode of 'Pimp My Ride', Gangsta gets to hang around shiny new cars all day, waxing lyrical about hubcaps and sound systems. The lack of girls draped across the bonnets is annoying, but at least he gets to see Caprice at the Motor Show every year.

COULD I
Be a Gangsta?

Living with a Gangsta is hard, but you tough it out.

Determined to understand your beloved Gangsta's world, you start to listen to a little gangsta rap yourself. You find it provides a handy outlet for your anger and you admire its simple ethos of bigger and better (you'd like a new kitchen, for example). You realise your clothes are not nearly expensive enough and your booty is a little stiff. So you go shopping, shed your sensible image and turn the music up. It feels so liberating. Respec'! Who's da gangsta now, huh, sucka?